Original title:
Life and Other Questions You're Not Supposed to Ask

Copyright © 2025 Creative Arts Management OÜ
All rights reserved.

Author: Liam Sterling
ISBN HARDBACK: 978-1-80566-261-7
ISBN PAPERBACK: 978-1-80566-556-4

The Width of Wonder

In a world where socks go missing,
Do they dance or just get shy?
I ponder on this quirky mystery,
With a laugh and a sigh.

Do cookies crumble when they're sad?
Or do they just want a friend?
Each bite feels like a question,
That the baker may not intend.

An Investigation of the Unseen

Why do we yell at our TVs?
Do they even hear our plight?
Those characters never listen,
It's a baffling, funny sight.

What secrets do cats conceal?
A world where dogs only dream?
Are they sharing their wild tales?
Or just plotting to scream?

Yearnings for Hidden Truths

When I finally lose the remote,
Is it hiding or just been found?
Do pillows feel my lost hopes?
Or just snore softly, profound?

What if socks had a secret club,
Where they plot to stay away?
And every time I search for one,
They're on a vacation day?

The Labyrinth of What-ifs

If bananas could talk, what would they say?
"Peel me with care, please!" they'd plead.
Do they gossip about apples?
While we nibble at their greed.

Would fish prefer land or the sea?
Swimming seems like such a bore.
What if turtles can actually fly?
But they're too cool to explore?

When the Clock Stops Ticking

When the clock stops, time takes a break,
We ponder our futures, and what paths we make.
Do seconds really matter, or is it just a game?
Stopping for snacks, we find fortune and fame.

With a tick and a tock, your sandwich is gone,
But my quest for cheese will always carry on!
I question the universe, while munching my fries,
Maybe the answer is hidden in pies!

Secrets Tucked in Corners

In every dark nook, a secret resides,
Like the socks that go missing, oh where do they hide?
Whispers of wisdom from dust bunnies' throne,
Teach us to laugh at the chaos we've sown.

With a broom in my hand, I launch my best scoff,
For every lost thing, a new life will scoff.
My cat seems to know every shadow's true jest,
But I just laugh harder, not taking a rest.

The Weight of Unasked Why's

Why do we ponder the puzzling and strange?
Like why we seek answers, but our cats still act deranged?

Each question like weights tied to my toes,
When asked of the universe, it giggles and glows.

Should we just skip worries, dive into the fun?
Go chocolate hunting, and say, 'Aren't we all one?'
With a wink and a nod, let's roll with the tide,
For clarity's overrated, let chaos be our guide!

Reflections in a Dusty Mirror

Gazing in mirrors coated with dust,
I see my reflection, it's a bit of a must.
Is that wisdom I'm seeing, or last night's dessert?
Either way, let's laugh while we wear our best shirt!

The truth sometimes hides in the fluff and the glare,
Like mismatched socks and the static in hair.
Let's toast to the riddles that make us all wise,
For every cracked image tells tales of surprise!

The Heartbeat of Uncertainty

In a world where socks are never paired,
The answers hide, a game well-played.
Why do we dance when the music's wrong?
We grin and hum, to carry on strong.

With questions bursting like bubbles of foam,
We ponder where all the lost keys roam.
Do cats really plot to take over the world?
Or just sharpen claws while their flags unfurled?

So grab your hat and join the spree,
Where queries bloom like a wild daisy.
Laughter's the compass when lost in the fray,
As we tumble through winks of the absurd every day.

Burdened by Curiosity

Why does toast always land buttered side down?
What's hidden beneath the old couch's crown?
Do fish have deep thoughts when they silently swim?
Or is every splash merely on a whim?

Why do we drive on parkways and park on the street?
Is cereal just soup you don't need to heat?
When eggs try to hatch, do they ever complain?
Or just roll with the punches, like life on a train?

With restless minds and eyes all aglow,
We search for the truth in the ebb and flow.
Giggles abound, as we tumble and sway,
Through riddles and musings that brighten our day.

Unspoken Whispers

In the silence, secrets giggle and chime,
Whispers of worries, but oh, what a rhyme!
Why do we worry about things that can't be?
Like if clouds hold up all the dreams we see.

Do vegetables speak when we're not around?
Or just plot their escape deep in the ground?
Why are adults so serious, stuck in a grind?
When the best answers hide in the childlike mind?

So let quirky musings bring joy to the chase,
As we skip through our thoughts in a whimsical race.
With laughter as fuel, we'll ponder with glee,
In the spaces between the absurd and the free.

The Curiosity Chronicles

Chasing shadows where questions abide,
We crack up at quirks we're typically shy.
What if time's just an elaborate trick?
Tick-tock on the wall says, 'Take your pick!'

What happens to missing socks in the wash?
Do they form a union, or maybe just squosh?
Why do we smile at the silliest things?
Like the antics of cats and the joy that they bring?

With minds like balloon animals tied in a knot,
We pop out ideas from the place where we're not.
So grab your laughter and let's take a ride,
Through the curious dances that we cannot hide.

Questions Beneath the Surface

Why do socks vanish in the wash?
Do they form a rogue colony?
Maybe they hold a secret dance,
Wearing shoes is just a form of tyranny.

What if plants can hear our thoughts?
Do they giggle when we fail?
I bet they mock our table scraps,
As they chat on the leafy trail.

Is the fridge really judging me?
Or is it just the light that's bright?
I hear it hum a soothing tune,
When I reach for snacks at night.

Can you skip life's awkward phases?
Or do they come with every year?
Like bad haircuts or strange outfits,
Embrace it all with a quirky cheer!

When Silence Gives Birth

In crowded rooms, what's the sound?
Is it laughter or just my sigh?
Fingers tapping, thoughts colliding,
Are we all just waiting to fly?

What's with the awkward small talk?
Do we practice in the mirror?
When I say 'nice weather, huh?',
Am I trying to sound sincere?

At the party, where's my drink?
Did I drop it or does it hide?
Is my sanity sinking low?
Or is this just a wild ride?

When the music starts to fade,
Do we dance to fill the void?
Or sit and question our existence,
While our hopes and dreams get toyed?

The Things We Never Say

What if cats plot our demise?
With their charming little purrs?
In their eyes, a calculating gaze,
While we think they're just fur blurs.

What's the story behind that pick?
The one from your awkward teen phase?
Do we laugh or cringe in silence,
As nostalgia sets the world ablaze?

Do dogs ever wish they could speak?
Or do they know all that we hide?
Each bark a mystery unraveling,
While we mask our hearts inside.

Why is it so hard to confess?
The small things that make us mere fools?
Like how I dance when no one sees,
Defining happiness by broken rules!

Queries of a Wandering Soul

What's the map of dreams we chart?
Is it written in stars above?
Or just doodles on a page,
With sticky notes that smell of love?

Do pets wonder where we go?
When we leave for just a while?
Do they hold a vigil of sorts?
Counting minutes with a smile?

If I ask the questions loud,
Will the universe reply back?
Would it wink and tap my shoulder,
Playing tricks on this time-worn track?

In the chase of daily grind,
Do we fly or simply drift?
As the clock ticks on our dreams,
What's the true and lasting gift?

The Time Between Answers

In the pause where echoes dwell,
Jokes are whispered, stories to tell.
Where silence stretches like a rubber band,
The clock makes faces, never quite planned.

Questions swirl like leaves in the breeze,
Tickling the brain, aiming to tease.
Wit dances around, just out of reach,
While the answer runs off to a speech.

Defying the Mundane

Morning coffee in mismatched cups,
Socks that never meet, poor little pups.
A dance with dust bunnies under the bed,
As we plot the day's grand mislead.

The toaster pops; it's a grand parade,
Each crumb a soldier, bold and made.
With breakfast served on a wobbly tray,
We conquer the world in our own funny way.

Beneath the Surface Shine

Mirrors lie, they don't reflect,
A smile's a mask, love's not perfect.
Underneath the shiny glaze,
A dance of chaos begins to blaze.

Peering deep, past the painted cheer,
The truth is jammed in the atmosphere.
We poke and prod at what we see,
Laughing at how odd our lives can be.

The Very Fabric of Wonder

Thread by thread, we weave our dreams,
In patterns full of quirky schemes.
Stitching giggles into the seams,
With a needle that's sharper than it seems.

A fabric patched with heart and care,
Dances boldly, wears our flair.
Forever questioning, we'll never tire,
Unraveling threads of thought in fire.

Secrets Wrapped in Silence

In the garden of whispers, secrets play,
Like cats on rooftops, they dance and sway.
With a wink and a nod, the gossip flies,
While the wise wear a grin, with knowing sighs.

Behind closed doors, the truth may lurk,
Yet in silly masks, we still go berserk.
Laughter spills forth, a mix of delight,
As we ponder our quirks, deep into the night.

The Depths of Curiosity

Why do socks vanish in the washing machine?
They plot with the missing crayons, it seems.
With questions like these, we spiral away,
   Into rabbit holes where oddities play.

Do fish ever wonder what's under the waves?
Or do they just swim and grin like brave knaves?
As we dig through the layers of silly and weird,
We find that the questions can never be cleared.

Half-formed Thoughts in Twilight

In twilight's embrace, ideas take flight,
With half-formed thoughts dancing in sight.
A pizza could solve many issues tonight,
While stars in the sky giggle, oh what a sight!

What if chairs could gossip about who sits?
And pillows just whisper our most secret bits?
In the soft glow of dusk, absurdities bloom,
As we question the strange, in the comforting room.

Explorations of the Uncharted

Let's set sail on the sea of the strange,
Where toast is the captain, ready for change.
What lies beyond the edge of the bed?
An exciting world of mismatched bread!

With quirks and oddities, we navigate bold,
In the uncharted waters, laughter unfolds.
Silly maps and treasures await our delight,
As we chart a course through the starry night.

The Art of Unspoken Thoughts

In a room full of chatter,
A silence hangs like a bat;
Do they think I'm a thinker?
Or just a quiet cat?

With a grin, I observe,
The chaos swirling around;
Do they know I'm the chef?
Of this silence I've found?

A question pops like a bubble,
But it's locked up tight;
To ask why cats have nine lives,
Seems a tad too contrite.

So I sip my cold drink,
And nod like a sage;
In the land of unasked queries,
I just waltz off the stage.

Beneath the Velvet Mask

Underneath this fine cover,
I'm more than meets the eye;
But ask me about the weather,
And I might just defy.

With a wink and soft chuckle,
I dance through the lies;
But deep down in my pockets,
Are the truths I disguise.

What's the secret of knowledge?
Oh, it's just a prank;
I made it up with bright colors,
And tossed it in the tank.

As the masquerade twirls,
With truths all intertwined;
I wear my velvet mask,
While the wisdom's maligned.

Chasing Echoes of Reality

In the hallways of nonsense,
I lose my sense of time;
Yet whispers of reason tease me,
With a jingle and rhyme.

But every time I ask why,
The echoes laugh in glee;
Reality's but a shadow,
Hiding somewhere, you see!

I chase it with a lollipop,
And a grin that won't fade;
Each question I throw at the wall,
Turns to confetti parade.

So let's frolic in madness,
And sip tea with the sly;
For chasing these echoes,
Is a glorious lie.

The Forbidden Inquiry

Hushed whispers fill the air,
As I ponder what's unsaid;
Why's there a sock on the ceiling?
Should it go with the bread?

I raise an eyebrow in wonder,
But nobody dares to ask;
Perhaps it's a sock puppet,
In an unlicensed mask?

Every question's a pickle,
Sitting snug on the shelf;
To reveal all the answers,
Is to unearth myself.

So here I stand quite silent,
With my thoughts in a stew;
The forbidden inquiry blooms,
In a garden of 'who knew?'

Whispers in the Unasked

Why do socks fade at great speeds,
While they vanish like magic indeed?
The dryer must be a portal to space,
Where lonely socks find a new place.

Jellybeans in colors so bright,
But which flavor is truly a fright?
Norms of taste often get crossed,
Who knew raspberry could taste like gloss?

What happens to old phones and keys?
Are they all plotting down there with bees?
Invisible parties in the dark,
With dances that start with a spark.

Is it too late for wishing on dimes?
Or do they count like some nursery rhymes?
Coins in fountains must hold deep schemes,
Telling fortunes in swirls and dreams.

The Curiosity of Shadows

Shadows flit like gossiping friends,
In shapes and sizes that twist and bend.
Why do they sneak away in the light,
And return with secrets, oh what a sight?

Do shadows dream of being seen,
In shades of purple, blue or green?
Perhaps they plot to overshadow us,
But it's hard to tell if it's all just fuss.

If I trip over my untied lace,
Does my shadow laugh or hide its face?
Does it ever wonder where I roam,
Or is it content just to call me home?

Will the night bring more shadowed fun,
When no one's around and the day is done?
Beneath the moon, do they dance and sway,
Conversing in tones of twilight play?

When Silence Speaks

When my cat stares without a sound,
Is she pondering things that astound?
Does she ponder the meaning of treats,
Or where the laser pointer retreats?

In the quiet, where thoughts collide,
What secrets do we often hide?
Is the fridge a confidant of sorts,
Where leftovers tell tales of food courts?

Why do we shush in movie halls,
As if whispers might break down the walls?
Is the popcorn really a spy,
Reporting all secrets with a crunch or sigh?

When laughter bubbles, is it for real?
Or just a mask we all conceal?
In silence, the smiles begin to gleam,
As questions bob on the surface of dreams.

Beneath the Surface of Normalcy

Beneath the calm of morning dew,
Are pancakes plotting, who knew?
Do eggs conspire to be the best,
While bacon lounges, taking a rest?

When the sun rises, what do plants say?
Do they gossip about the clouds on display?
"Did you see how the wind took that leave?"
In the world of green, they never believe.

What goes on in lines at the store?
Do carts hold debates or simply bore?
Behind the scenes, transactions so sly,
Is the cashier a wizard in disguise?

Normalcy's cover is thin, they say,
Mundane mischief reigns day by day.
If we peeked underneath, oh what a surprise,
The ordinary world wears a comical guise.

Hidden Dialogues

Whispers dance in dusty halls,
As socks debate the missing pairs.
Is it fate or just the laundry?
Oh, the secrets it declares.

The plants gossip about your mood,
While the cat rolls its eyes in disdain.
Do we really know who's in charge?
Or is it all just a clever game?

Coffee cups converse with the spoon,
Sharing dreams of sugar and cream.
Do they know that we eavesdrop?
Or are we lost in our own steam?

Life's a stage with a jester's hat,
Where questions arise like magic tricks.
Who wrote the script for this circus?
Good luck finding the perfect flick!

The Unseen Pathways

The fridge hums a tune of delight,
While the leftovers plot their escape.
Do they dream of greener pastures?
Or just some fantasy on a grape?

Shoes left by the door have a meeting,
Discussing where they should tread.
One wants to climb a mountain high,
While another just dreams of the bed.

The couch cushions have seen it all,
Witnessing dramas of snacks and sighs.
Who knew such comfy seats held secrets?
Or was that just last night's fries?

A calendar hangs, a mockingly grin,
As days blur into nothingness.
What did we really plan for today?
Just another game of "Guess Who's Guess?"

Pondering Under Moonlight

Beneath the moon's sarcastic smile,
I ponder where socks vanish.
Are they hosting a grand parade?
Or just having a ninja's banish?

The stars twinkle with a knowing wink,
As owls chatter in wise old tones.
Do they judge our midnight snacks?
Or are they just watching our phones?

What if wishes fall like rain?
Would umbrellas catch our hopes?
Or are they simply drenched in dreams,
Hoping for luck in slippery slopes?

Counting sheep turns into a riot,
As they argue on the way to sleep.
"Not this week! That's a busy night!"
While I just chuckle and weep.

The Echo of Untold Stories

In the attic, dust collects the tales,
Of forgotten toys on wooden shelves.
Do they giggle under dust motes?
Or craft stories where they're themselves?

The books on the shelf plot new journeys,
While ghosts of authors sip their tea.
Are they laughing at our book clubs?
Or mocking the plots that we'll see?

The clock ticks with a wise old nod,
Counting seconds, yet feigning pauses.
Does it know our hesitations?
Or just loves to toy with our causes?

Life's a riddle wrapped in laughter,
As we scribble ideas on the breeze.
Will we find the punchline someday?
Or just revel in the mysteries?

The Edge of Realization

On the brink of a thought, I stare,
Does the toaster toast more love than air?
The fridge hums a tune quite divine,
But does it dream of grapes or wine?

In the hall of my mind, a ghost does slide,
With existential sneakers, it takes a ride.
Shall I chase it down the rabbit hole?
Or sit with my snack and just scroll?

Navigating the Great Unknown

With a compass that spins, I venture wide,
Seeking answers that I can't decide.
Is it the sock's fault I've lost the pair?
Or just my living room's smelly affair?

Navigating dreams laced with cheese,
My pillow asks, "What's the purpose, please?"
But visions of pizza cloud my view,
So I settle on napping for something new.

Eclipsed by Questions

Why do ducks quack and not sing a tune?
What's the secret of the moon's silver spoon?
I asked a cat, but it just stared,
As if my thoughts were simply impaired.

The laundry keeps piling, but why must it?
Every sock's a mystery, just like my wit.
In a world full of emojis and memes,
I ponder if laughter hides in my dreams.

Unraveling Truths Yet Unseen

A puzzle of life, so jumbled and bright,
Like cereal boxes lost in the night.
Is gravity just a polite little lie?
Or is it the reason my muffin won't fly?

I asked my plants if they felt the sun,
They nodded, but then forgot the fun.
With mysteries stacked on top of my bed,
I giggle and muse, 'What's next on the thread?'

Fleeting Glimpses of Truth

In the fridge, I found my dreams,
Hiding behind leftover beans.
They winked at me in bright neon,
"Don't forget, you're not alone!"

The cat judged, perched on high,
Musing why I eat that pie.
As if her life is pure and neat,
Chasing shadows with tiny feet.

My toaster pops in warning shouts,
"You're burning toast, not solving doubts!"
Bread crumbs scatter like lost thoughts,
In this kitchen of wild plots.

I asked a plant if it can feel,
It leafed me off; was that a deal?
Silent truths with giggles wrapped,
Whispering secrets, slightly napped.

The Path of Unsung Questions

Why do socks always lose their pairs?
They wander off without much cares.
The dryer spins their tales so bold,
Leaving me with stories untold.

Each morning brings a brand new quest,
Is coffee brewed by magic press?
I ponder deep while sipping slow,
Is caffeine the key to know?

The clock ticks loud, like laughter's game,
Why rush when time's a silly fame?
I stand perplexed, with no clear view,
As time suggests I'm overdue.

With questions, I play hide-and-seek,
In corners where the answers peak.
I find that reason takes a nap,
In paradox, I gladly trap.

Moments of Uncertainty

I stepped outside to face the day,
Tripped on hopes that got in the way.
Clouds chuckled, the sun just grinned,
What's ahead? Will I win or sin?

A bird sang off-key to the sky,
"Embrace the chaos, why not try?"
With each note, I felt less sure,
Laughing at paths that blur and purr.

The grass grew tall and waved hello,
Inviting me to forget my woe.
With every step, confusion blooms,
A mixed bouquet of doubts and tunes.

People march with grand designs,
While I scribble on napkin lines.
With questions sprouting up like weeds,
In uncertainty, curiosity feeds.

Explorations Beyond Reason

In the attic, where old thoughts lie,
Dust bunnies grin and wonder why.
Are dreams made of fabric or air?
I question, while vintage chairs stare.

The map to logic crumples in folds,
Revealing treasures of stories untold.
Are we really on a quest so grand?
Or just wandering in search of sand?

The neighbor's dog thinks he knows best,
Barking orders as if it's a test.
Between wise cracks and silly barks,
I ponder how to dodge the sparks.

What if answers played hide-and-seek?
And giggles wrapped the philosophique?
In this dance of goofy whim,
I'll chase the absurd, on a whim.

Chasing Shadows of Doubt

In the corner of my mind, they play,
Shadows whispering, leading astray.
Should I wear red shoes or blue?
Decisions to make, oh what's a fool to do?

Should I ask the cat where to go?
She just purrs and steals the show.
Perhaps a map made of cheese?
But do mice ever do as they please?

Beneath the Marmalade Skies

Beneath skies painted toast with jam,
Birds discuss the latest scam.
Why do they croon? What's the score?
Are they trading stocks or just wanting more?

Clouds like cotton candy fluff,
Is life a treat, or is it tough?
Why do we laugh at silly things?
While a cactus secretly dreams of wings?

Contemplating the Forbidden

Do socks really match, or is that a ruse?
While some wear colors, others choose blues.
Is cereal soup, in a morning trance?
Should pancakes twirl, or just cha-cha dance?

Do goldfish gossip in their little bowls?
Or plot their escape like crafty trolls?
Questions swirl in the bubbling brew,
But who really knows what's right and true?

The Curiosity of Existence

Why do we wake up to greet the day?
With alarm clocks shouting, "Hey! Hey! Hey!"
Do trees gossip about the sun?
While squirrels debate who's more fun?

Can a duck know the purpose of flight?
Or a sofa ponder what's wrong or right?
Perhaps the stars keep their secrets deep,
As we search for answers in the cosmic sweep.

Truths Entwined in Nightmares

In dreams, I find a talking cat,
He spills the beans on what I'm at.
He knows my foibles, what's more,
The socks I hide behind the door.

In shadows lurk my soggy toast,
Each bite I take, a ghostly boast.
A dance with crumbs beneath my bed,
What's lost, what's found? We can't be fed.

The Dilemma of Silence

When I don't speak, my thoughts run wild,
   A circus troupe, oh, what a child!
    In every pause, a hidden jest,
   Will laughter come, or be a pest?

The clock ticks loud like thunder's rift,
   I ponder hard, oh what a gift!
    Am I a sage or just a fool?
   At least I still can break the rule.

Fleeting Moments of Clarity

Sometimes I see the world so clear,
Like clouds that part, bring on the cheer.
But then a sock inside the fridge,
Reminds me just how things can smidge.

A pop quiz waits on Tuesday morn,
With questions dressed in woes forlorn.
Who stole my coffee? Such a mess!
A mystery wrapped in tiredness.

Whims of the Unwritten

With pen in hand, I sway and spin,
My stories hide, they grip, they grin.
A page not turned, but tea gone cold,
What mischief waits in tales untold?

The sun can rise, or just pretend,
Each plot twist bends, will it offend?
I scribble lines that dance about,
In worlds of thoughts, I twist and shout.

Navigating the Improbable

In a world where ducks wear hats,
We ponder how they sit on mats.
The sun may rise from the sea,
But does it really care for me?

A cat once ordered a cheeseburger,
In a diner that had no urge for.
We laugh at the wildest sight,
Is it wrong to dream at night?

While waiting for toast to toast,
We wonder who makes the most boast.
Is it better to follow or lead?
Or simply enjoy every misdeed?

Perhaps a raccoon can explain,
Why we try to dodge the rain.
With peanut butter on our shoes,
We dance to the rhythm of blues.

The Paradox of Knowing

Why do socks always go astray?
Like wisdom that keeps the world at bay.
The more we seek, the less we find,
Like trying to persuade a blind cat to mind.

In a bubble where logic bursts,
We drink from wells of our own thirsts.
What if people were just five feet tall?
Would we still worry about it all?

The fridge hums secrets it can't share,
Maybe cheese is the wise one there.
If knowledge were a pair of shoes,
Would we still wear mismatched hues?

A squirrel debates with a passing breeze,
About the benefits of cracked walnuts with ease.
Do we learn or just pretend to know?
As the toaster finally steals the show.

At the Edge of Certainty

At the edge of a garden gnome,
We question our choice of a home.
Is the grass truly greener over there?
Or do lawnmowers just seem to care?

When thoughts collide like fruit in a stew,
Do we blend them or stick with a few?
A dog once tried to teach me math,
But only got lost in its own path.

In dreams, we ride on flamingos bright,
While pondering whether it's day or night.
Does advice come wrapped in silly hats?
Or born from pondering the quirks of cats?

With every question tossed like a ball,
We chase after echoes, heed the call.
If certainty wore polka dot shoes,
Would it dance to the rhythm of news?

Curves of Intrigue

In a world that spins like a topsy toy,
We search for meaning and some joy.
What if fish learned to fly,
Would that make the cat say good-bye?

A pizza slice can sometimes explain,
Why we all go a bit insane.
When jellybeans argue on the ground,
Does the truth lie where they're found?

Curves of intrigue twist and twine,
While butterflies sip on sweet lemonade wine.
Do we choose to laugh or simply frown?
In a game where everyone wears a crown?

Mice in tuxedos dance on the floor,
Teaching us things we can't ignore.
When questions swirl like leaves in fall,
Can we dance to the laughter, after all?

Shadows of Inquiry

Why do socks vanish in the wash?
Is there a sock thief lurking?
Do forks and spoons conspire late?
While the kitchen's tunes keep chirping?

What's the flavor of invisible soup?
Can cats really plot our doom?
Why do we laugh at dad jokes still?
Hoping not to meet that vacuum's broom?

Is the closet a portal to weird lands?
Do kitchen tiles hold secret plans?
Why do we never see the shoe?
While the left-hand foot silently stands?

Whose idea was the round cookie?
To fit them in a square box too?
When questions rise like bread in the heat,
We giggle—pretending we never knew.

Forbidden Curiosities

Why do we fear the bathroom scale?
It tells the secrets we'd rather fail.
Is the rumor true about your taste buds?
That they applaud every morsel we inhale?

Do plants have secret life goals too?
Plotting world takeover, what can they do?
The houseplants whisper by the window,
Dreaming of greater things to pursue.

Why do we name computers with pride?
As if they'll help when we lose our ride?
Can my toaster critique my breakfast?
Or just sit there—an idle guide?

Is the chair you sit in just lazy?
Acting as if it's all a bit hazy?
Do they swap places when we're away?
Rearranging plans, am I just crazy?

Echoes in the Void

What's the source of a sneeze, I wonder?
Is it really just dust that's under?
Do our noses tell lies as they twitch?
While our brains play a game of blunder?

Do shadows stretch just to tease?
Or do they dance to a silent breeze?
Is there a shadow union in talk?
Chasing light like the greatest thieves?

Can coffee understand human woes?
And do crayons envy our prose?
Why does chocolate mend a broken heart?
With each sugary nod, it surely knows.

Do we paint our lives with checkered hues?
As if life's a puzzle with no clues?
Or are we merely sketches in time?
Each stroke making up the various views?

The Mystery of Unasked Thoughts

If my sandwich could talk, what would she say?
Pickles with attitudes, 'Hey, eat me today!'
Do ants hold conferences on pie crumbs?
As they scheme their gourmet buffet?

Do mirrors reflect more than just hair?
What secrets hide when no one's there?
Are we all just actors on stage?
In the drama of the unaware?

What's the deal with that lone parking space?
Is it saving seats or just showing grace?
Can you hear laughter in an empty room?
Or is it eavesdropping at work, just in case?

When clouds gather, do they plot?
To sprinkle joy, or take a shot?
Is every rainbow the end of a quest?
For answers we never ever thought?

Threads of Uncertainty

In the laundry of thoughts, I find,
Socks and dreams, all intertwined.
Who shrank my hopes? Or did they flee,
Escaping into the abyss of spree?

My toaster's a philosopher, I swear,
Toasts me wisdom when I'm unaware.
But what's the crust? What's the fluff?
Pondering toasters just aren't enough.

I ask my cat, for sage advice,
She stares at me, thinks I'm not nice.
Her answer's a yawn, a stretch, a sigh,
Oh well, I'll just try the pie in July.

Then there's the fridge, cold and true,
It whispers secrets of what we chew.
Should I snack, or should I fast?
It tells me to wait, like a wizard, aghast.

Musings on the Edge of Reason

Why do we drive on the right and not the left?
Is it a choice, or just a theft?
My GPS mocks me with every turn,
Lost in the woods, did I fail to learn?

The chicken crossed, but where's the beef?
Is there meaning in this comic relief?
Eating salad, I question my fate,
Are vegetables friends, or just on a plate?

With coffee brewed strong, I gingerly sit,
Counting all the bills that don't seem to fit.
A penny saved? A penny lost!
What's the cost of being a boss?

And as my plants thrive on neglect,
I wonder if they too feel the wreck.
Green leaves whisper, "You could try,"
But my thumbs are brown, oh me, oh my!

The Questions We Bathe In

Splashing water, bubbles rise,
Do ducks float in endless skies?
I ponder shampoo, why do we care?
Do they conspire with conditioner in there?

Why must I scrub to feel brand new?
Every wash feels like déjà vu.
I sing a tune to distract my mind,
But what's the meaning in suds so blind?

The rubber duck, wise and bright,
Judges my soap with all its might.
Do you think it knows I miss my socks?
Or is it just gloating in the blocks?

With every rinse, questions remain,
Like soap scum on the window pane.
I'll lather on, and laugh out loud,
In this bathtub circus, I feel proud!

Footprints Through the Fog

Walking in fog, each step's a guess,
Where am I going? Who's to impress?
The trees nod gently, lost in the haze,
Their branches whisper of staggering ways.

Footprints lead where? A maze I see,
Is it wisdom, or just a plea?
With every shuffle, I feel more alive,
Tripping on answers that won't quite arrive.

The world's a puzzle, but who fits where?
In foggy moments, there's plenty to share.
Each laugh floats freely, a wisp on the air,
Even if some crumbs haven't gone anywhere.

So here I dance through shadows and cheer,
With questions that tickle, and dreams that leer.
The fog may thicken, but my spirit won't lag,
In this whimsical journey, I wave my flag!

The Quest for Unseen Landscapes

Why do socks vanish in the wash?
Are they off to a sock party? Oh the posh!
The dust bunnies roam beneath the bed,
Plotting world takeovers, all while we're fed.

Do we ever find the remote control?
Or does it hike up to a distant stroll?
It's a mystery wrapped in a cushion's fluff,
While we search with faces all huffed and gruff.

The cat stares at walls with such intent,
Is she plotting a scheme or simply content?
Her glance holds secrets of realms untold,
In her kingdom of chaos, she's brazen and bold.

Yet here we stand with questions galore,
Should we ask or just ignore?
For in this quest, we laugh and we sigh,
The unseen landscapes are why we all try.

Murmurs Beneath the Surface

What's that sound from the fridge at night?
A ghostly hum or a leftover's fright?
It calls to the milk like a siren's song,
Yet in the morning, we ponder, 'What's wrong?'

The plants whisper gossip when we don't look,
'Is that a new leaf?' They quietly crook,
Spying on us while we're glued to screens,
Their leafy lives are filled with dreams.

In deep conversations with the bathroom scale,
It giggles softly, 'You really won't fail!'
As numbers dance at their own merry pace,
We calmed our palpitations, hiding disgrace.

So we chuckle and shrug at the strange little things,
The murmurs below, oh what joy it brings!
For as we tread softly on this odd ground,
Together we laugh at the mysteries found.

Whispers of Enigma

Why is cereal so loud in the bowl?
It crackles and pops like it's out of control.
With each crunchy bite, the milk doth sway,
Are they plotting to sing? Oh, what do they say?

The coffee pot brews with a mystical tune,
As it dances with steam under the light of the moon,
Each cup holds a riddle, a secret or two,
About mornings we dread, yet still we pursue.

What is it with traffic lights in the mist?
Do they laugh at us all or simply insist?
We question the cosmos at the end of the day,
While dreaming of being somewhere far away.

In the midst of the chaos, the whispers remain,
Tickling our minds like a soft summer rain.
With enigmas around us, we shuffle and sway,
Finding humor in answers that shift andelay.

Brushing Against the Infinite

Why do chairs seem to know our name?
Each time we sit, it's all just the same.
They twirl and spin in an elusive dance,
As we ponder their motives in a comical trance.

The tick-tock of clocks feels oddly like jazz,
They're grooving to time while we simply stare, pizzazz.
Do they scoff at our haste, our frantic chase?
With every tick, they smile and embrace.

What's the deal with old pennies we find?
They hold stories unwritten, of time intertwined.
Wishing wells whisper secrets they keep,
While we laugh at the wishes, forgetting to weep.

So we brush against moments, both silly and grand,
In a world where absurdity forever will stand.
Together we roam through the quirks and the spins,
Finding joy in the random, that's where it begins.

The Weight of Words Unspoken

In silence we barter, like fish in a stream,
A whisper of thoughts that do not dare beam.
We laugh at the questions that dance in our heads,
While pondering whether to talk or to thread.

The weight of the tales that we bury inside,
Can puff up a heart, like a balloon in the tide.
With each fleeting chuckle, we dodge the deep quest,
As we sip on our coffee and play at our best.

Yet giggles ensue when we glimpse at the truth,
Unwrapped in a moment, it springs like a sleuth.
We ponder on whether to shout or to sigh,
As banter and curiosity stroll on by.

So raise your mugs high to the secrets we keep,
In this comical circus, we'll never lose sleep.
For every unspoken carries a jest,
And laughter's the answer, we jest with the rest.

Whims of Enigmatic Answers

Questions like bubbles rise up from the deep,
With answers that wiggle, yet often just creep.
In the blur of the quizzical, we play hide and seek,
As wisdom wears jammies and refuses to speak.

A riddle of sorts, we clamor to solve,
While answers grow weary, and troubles dissolve.
The fortune teller's gaze is a funny charade,
With tarot of giggles that barely invade.

What's the reason for socks that don't match?
Is there logic to labels our brains try to hatch?
Upon asking, we find we've created a jest,
As we roll in the puns that fit none but the best.

So let's toast to the madness of questions galore,
Each whimsy spins wildly, leaving us wanting more.
In a world full of puzzles, don't search for a stance,
But dance with the silly, and give it a chance.

Soliloquies for the Inquisitive

In shadows we ponder, with quirks on display,
Questions take flight like confetti in May.
A soliloquy spills from a curious heart,
While laughter looks on, it's a fanciful art.

Each ponderous thought wears a comical cap,
As we sing our doubts like a jazzy mishap.
Why do ducks quack? Or the sky wear a frown?
The answers seem lost in the circus of clowns.

We twirl with the riddles, each spin brings a grin,
In the tapestry woven, the mischief begins.
With musings unshackled, we glide on a sweep,
Finding joy in the questions, no answers to keep.

So raise up your voices to chatter and play,
In this whimsical banquet, let's merrily stay.
For every inquiry holds a riddle so fine,
And in laughter's embrace, we eternally shine.

Approaching the Unapproachable

Like whispers in twilight, we tiptoe with flair,
Toward questions that dangle like leaves in the air.
The unapproachable beckons, with shadows so wide,
Yet giggles persist in the truth we can't hide.

With every bold step, we stumble and trip,
On answers that shiver, and teeter on lip.
What's the secret of socks that keep going alone?
Or why do we fear what we seldom have shown?

In jest we seek reasons, like fish on a line,
Unraveling knots in our thoughts over time.
So why not embrace all the whims we can find,
As we chuckle and wander, with questions entwined?

Let's dance with the strange, let absurdity reign,
In a world filled with wonders, we'll gather the gain.
For every wild question invites a good laugh,
And wisdom's a trickster that loves to outdraft.

Layers Beneath the Calm

In the stillness of a pond,
Fish debate their lunch plans.
Bubbles rise like secrets shared,
While frogs croak their loud demands.

The trees gossip in the breeze,
Whispering tales of ant escapades.
Squirrels plot heists for the acorns,
As bees dance in their ballets.

The clouds wear masks of innocence,
While rainbows arch with sneaky glee.
Nature juggles odd curiosities,
Yet pretends it's all carefree.

Beneath the calm, a circus roams,
Unseen beneath the surface veil.
It's clear the world's a funny show,
With giggles trapped in a fishy tale.

Secrets of the Unexplored

In a cupboard, dust collects,
Where mismatched socks become best friends.
A world of wonders unexplored,
Where loneliness makes no amends.

Old toys hold grudges in the dark,
Waiting for a child to play.
Forgotten whispers of adventures,
Echo down the aisle of yesterday.

The attic holds a grumpy ghost,
Who pouts beneath the cobwebs' lace.
Yet, when I bring snacks, he smiles wide,
Revealing secrets of the place.

In hidden nooks, the oddballs thrive,
As laughter leaps from shadowed beds.
Embrace the strange and unexplored,
For the funniest tales are often said.

Musings on the Edge

Perched upon a windy cliff,
Seagulls squawk their wise advice.
"What's the deal with gravity?"
"Why don't we all just flop like dice?"

Pondering why the stars align,
While socks hide in a cosmic whirl.
Why does pizza taste so great,
On nights when life feels like a twirl?

The ocean's waves have tales to tell,
Of mermaids trapped in tangled nets.
Yet, as I squint to see their dance,
I wonder why I'm place with bets.

Laughing with the wind, I muse,
What's the point of being sane?
On the edge, where thoughts collide,
It's fun to ponder, what's a brain?

The Art of Questioning Without Words

A raised brow can say it all,
Like signals tossed in fleeting glances.
Through the air, questions float,
Making people dance in their trances.

A side-eye here, a twitching lip,
Invites the mind to swirl and spin.
In silence, thoughts build a bridge,
Connecting laughter, without a din.

A shrug can squash the heaviest doubt,
As quirks convey the daily grind.
Who needs to shout when you can pout?
In wondering, the humor's blind.

The art of asking in silence thrives,
Creating chuckles from our scars.
It's witty how questions linger,
As music from the dancing stars.

Beyond the Surface Glance

Why did the chicken cross the street?
To question existence, not for a treat.
But humans stare, confused and lost,
As if pondering the chicken's cost.

Do ducks have dreams of flying high?
Or just quack tales without a sigh?
Philosophers muse with a furrowed brow,
But in the end, who really knows how?

A cat's nine lives, so widely known,
Yet they hold secrets, not a single tone.
With every leap on a sunny day,
Answering questions in a silly way.

So raise a glass to the curious minds,
To the silly questions that fate unwinds.
For in laughter, we find the clues,
To ponder deeply, but wear funny shoes.

The Intrigue of the Untouched

What's in the box? We'll never know,
Like socks that vanish, a funny show.
Is there a sock monster causing the mess?
Or just our forgetfulness, I must confess.

Why do birds sing at the break of dawn?
Do they plot revenge or simply yawn?
Maybe they're like us, just waiting to chat,
While staring at cats who silently sat.

Did the first person ever forget to smile?
Or was happiness just out of style?
Cuz laughter echoes in mystical ways,
Revealing the joy in our clumsy plays.

So here's to the things left unexplained,
The silly thoughts we've all entertained.
In the puzzling dance of the everyday,
We find humor, come what may.

Delving into the Unanswerable

If olives are fruit, then what's a nut?
Are hotdogs tacos in a clever rut?
Worlds collide with each curious bite,
As even our food holds the weight of the night.

What's the sound of one hand clapping loud?
Or the logic behind a confused crowd?
Questions spiral like a dog chasing tails,
Every answer found, another prevails.

If you open a can in the library,
Is it sound or silence that we should carry?
For in big questions, the small ones remain,
Like why can't we train our pet chicken to feign?

So ponder we shall, with a laugh or two,
At the riddles all around, and the strange things we do.
In this ultimate quest that's endlessly bright,
We dance in humor, embracing the light.

Unraveling Life's Puzzles

Why do we park on driveways, it's plain to see?
And why do we never talk to the TV?
These little quirks make us scratch our heads,
While trying to decode what logic dreads.

If a tree falls and no one is there,
Does it really fall, or is it just air?
With squirrels chattering, answers elude,
As we unravel the mysteries in a silly mood.

Are we really made of stardust, they say?
Or just room temp leftovers from yesterday?
In our quest to find what makes us tick,
We stumble through puzzles, with humor so thick.

So let's laugh at the riddles, the quirks, and the mess,
In the grand scheme of things, we're truly blessed.
With silly questions keeping our spirits afloat,
We wander this world, on a whimsical boat.

The Weight of Unuttered Worries

In the fridge, I seek my fate,
A pickle jar and thoughts await.
Should I eat, or just pretend?
These questions never seem to end.

Each cough and sneeze ignites my fear,
Is it flu, or just a sneeze, dear?
I check my pulse, the clock, the light,
Am I a hypochondriac tonight?

Do socks in pairs hold secret glee,
Or are they plotting just for me?
I wish they'd simply make their case,
And save me from this lonely space.

What if cats could speak, I muse,
Would they demand all our best views?
Or just discuss the weather spree,
And whether mice, in fact, have glee?

Contemplations in the Quiet

Alone at night, I find my thoughts,
In between my tangled knots.
What's the deal with bubble wrap?
Is it therapy, or just a trap?

The clock ticks loud, a ticking beast,
Is it a sign, or just a feast?
Should I dance or sit and stare,
At the shadows knotted in the air?

Why do we stare at life's small things,
Like spoons, or doors that don't have swings?
Do they hold secrets, ancient tales?
Or just remind us that we fail?

A goldfish swims in quiet grace,
In its bowl, the world's a race.
Do they ponder or just float?
In their world, there's no remote.

Thoughts That Dance in Darkness

In pitch black night, the echoes play,
Are they wise, or just cliché?
Why do shadows dance on walls?
Is it boredom that befalls?

The lightbulb flickers, quite a tease,
Does it feel the silent wheeze?
Should I replace it, take the risk?
Or wait until it's gone, then whisk?

What if clouds have secret lives,
Sipping tea while the world dives?
Do they gossip 'bout the sun's bright flare,
Or ponder why the moon's so rare?

I wonder if my cat knows it all,
Watches as my plans just stall.
Does she laugh when I trip and fall?
Or silently plot against my call?

Searching for Clarity in Chaos

A sock in the dryer spins alone,
Is it lost or just has grown?
What's the meaning of this fate?
Is there logic, or just debate?

Puzzles scattered on the floor,
Do they laugh when I implore?
Each piece misplaced or just a test,
Am I solving, or just a mess?

Whiskers twitch at the morning light,
Do cats dream of soaring flight?
Or contemplate the depth of time,
As they lounge in the sun, sublime?

Tomorrow's plans are quite absurd,
With lists so long, and all unheard.
Do we yearn for what we lack,
Or just retreat from all we rack?

Glances at the Improbable

Why does the toast always land down?
Is it a conspiracy from the town?
Cats plot in shadows, I'm sure of this,
While I just seek my morning bliss.

Do socks have a secret dance they do?
When they slip away, from your shoe?
The fridge hums, a wise sage at night,
Offering snacks till morning light.

What if the moon's a giant cheese wheel?
And astronauts are just looking for meal?
Grapes whisper secrets of the vine,
While I'm losing track of time.

In mirrors, do reflections plan schemes?
Or are they just stuck in daydreams?
Life's puzzle seems skewed and bent,
Yet laughter's the best form of rent.

The Quest for the Unknown

Is the dark really a friend in disguise?
Or just a place for dad's strange fries?
What lies beyond the laundry pile?
A treasure trove or just a while?

Can a goldfish ponder its own fate?
Or is it blissfully late for a date?
I wonder if plants discuss their woes,
Underneath all those watering rows.

If clouds had faces, would they smile?
Or pout for miles? Just a while?
Maybe they envy the ground that's firm,
While I just seek a fun little term.

What if time's a giant rubber band?
That stretches, twists, just not as planned?
With each tick, we trip and we giggle,
Chasing questions that always wiggle.

Pieces of a Broken Compass

Where does the other sock always go?
To a sock party? I want in, though!
Naps feel like mini time machines,
Where dreams are lost in crazy scenes.

What's the deal with mismatched spoons?
Do they gather for late-night tunes?
In the kitchen, chaos reigns supreme,
While I just try to live the dream.

Is gravity just a big prank we play?
Sending us tumbling every day?
Each trip and fall, a dance with fate,
I laugh it off, but who can say?

If only my thoughts came with a map,
To navigate this zany chap.
Yet here we are, afloat in a sea,
Searching for truth with giddy glee.

Gazing into the Abyss

What if the abyss just needs a hug?
And all it takes is a cheerful mug?
Do shadows gossip about our fate?
Or just munch on crumbs from our plate?

Can dreams be jealous of our snores?
Saying, "Hey, what about us, yours?"
Tangled in blankets, we drift away,
Wondering how to brighten our day.

If the unknown wore silly hats,
Would it dance with dogs and chat with cats?
Maybe the universe is just a game,
With cosmic players, none the same.

Do questions really have a safe place?
Or do they race at a breakneck pace?
In the end, it's a chaotic spree,
And laughter's the key to being free.

The Dance of Doubt and Truth

Two left feet on a dance floor,
Twisting thoughts, what's it all for?
Truth whispers sweetly, doubt takes a leap,
Who's leading? Oh, it's all just a sweep.

Round and round, they spin and twirl,
A confetti shower, a dizzying whirl.
Should I trust the waltz or tango with wit?
I'll just shuffle, can't figure this bit.

With every step, the questions fly,
Pondering why the truth can't lie.
Is it okay to laugh or to cry?
In this dance, we twist, we sigh.

So let's grab a friend, join the team,
In a world where we question our dreams.
With sighs and snickers, we'll find our groove,
In the dance of doubt, let's make our move.

Sketches of a Curious Mind

A crayon scribble on a blank page,
Thoughts bounce around like a jumping sage.
What if the sky turned a shade of green?
Would the sun throw a fit or just stay unseen?

Sketching questions with a cheeky grin,
Why is the cat always plotting a win?
Is the moon really cheese or just a charade?
I'd trade all my snacks for a solar parade!

Lines zigzag with laughter and glee,
Why do we fumble so endlessly?
In doodles of doubt and bursts of fun,
The curious mind thinks it's just begun.

With every scribble, stories unfold,
A canvas of wonder, brave and bold.
Let's color outside, no need to confine,
In sketches of madness, we're all intertwined!

Mapping the Unfathomable

With a paper map and a compass that spins,
I'm finding my way through a world full of sins.
Is the route here marked, or am I lost?
Navigating nonsense comes at a cost.

Dots on a surface, what do they mean?
X marks the spot, or so it would seem.
I chart all my worries, so carefully penned,
But the journey's the fun part, my dear, not the end!

What lies at the edge of this curious chart?
A treasure of laughter, a curious heart?
I'll draw on my map all the strange things I see,
Like that wandering gnome, sipping sweet tea.

So here's to the paths we might never explore,
Each twist and each turn just opens a door.
With crayons and laughter, we map out our way,
In the unfathomable, we frolic and play!

The Flicker of Hidden Insights

An old lamp flickers with secrets untold,
Hints of wisdom, both random and bold.
Why does it glow while the shadows creep?
In the dance of ideas, I feign a leap.

Jokes buried deep like treasures in sand,
What's the punchline? Do you understand?
With each playful flicker, the mind starts to race,
In the glow of the bulb, we're lost in the chase.

Questions pop up like popcorn in heat,
Each kernel a notion, so silly, yet sweet.
Is the answer tucked under the couch or a chair?
While finding the truth, I might just lose hair!

So let's breathe in the humor, let's embrace the confusion,

As light bends and dances, we'll watch the illusion.
In flickers of insights we laugh and we jest,
Finding joy in the riddles is surely the best!

Confessions of a Wanderer

I once asked a squirrel for directions,
But he just chattered and scurried away.
The map in my pocket felt like a curse,
As the trees laughed, begging me to stay.

A toaster didn't pop when I was so hungry,
It smiled and said, 'Patience is key.'
I pondered the meaning of breakfast bliss,
Over crumbs and burnt toast, where's the tea?

The shoes on my feet had traveled so far,
Yet here I am, stuck in this chair.
One more question, can I fly to the stars?
Or is that just a shoe sale I dreamily dare?

In my journal, I scribble some nonsense,
About how potatoes dance in the sun.
But deep down I know, it's all just a game,
So pass me the butter, we're having some fun.

Unraveled Threads of Existence

Why did the chicken cross over the moon?
Was she chasing some dreams, or avoiding the gloom?
The fabric of time seems so threadbare,
Yet here I am, still searching for my room.

Every cat I meet acts like they know,
The universe's secrets or where I should go.
I ask them politely, with treats on the line,
But they just stare blankly, as if they're in a show.

Coffee stains cover my morning thoughts,
Reminding me softly of battles I've fought.
The cup is half-empty; my mind leaves the scene,
Caffeine-fueled dreams and chaos I've sought.

The wind whispers tales of laughter and woe,
Am I just a speck in this wild, swirling flow?
With each whispered secret, I giggle and roam,
In this playful question mark, I've made my home.

The Spaces Between Words

In the spaces between, where silence hangs tight,
Are all the things said when we're too shy to bite.
I asked a goldfish about love and fate,
He swam in circles, said, 'Isn't it great?'

Grammar rules love to bend and to break,
Like a pretzel on days when I'm craving a cake.
Each comma and period feels like a tease,
As I write my confessions, like whispers to breeze.

A dictionary once tried to define my heart,
But it got too flustered and fell all apart.
Synonyms lounging, across pages like friends,
Offering cocktails of words that they send.

So here's to the spaces, so vast and so wide,
Where laughter and curiosity cheekily hide.
In between every sentence, let's dance and play,
For language is floppy, but oh what a way!

Questions Knocking in the Dark

What's that sound at the edge of my thought?
Is it wisdom or just the cat that I bought?
Each answer is hiding in shadows, they tease,
While I tiptoe softly, like a breeze through the trees.

Can the walls really listen, or is it my mind?
Echoes of laughter, or something unkind?
I clapped for the answers, but they never came,
Just a chorus of crickets, all singing the same.

Why do socks always vanish in the wash?
Is there a door to another dimension, a posh?
A universe filled with lonely lost items,
Where mismatched socks plot their bubbly rhymes.

So here's to the questions that dance in the night,
Knocking and laughing, oh what a delight!
With curiosity's lantern, let's wander afar,
For the funniest answers are never bizarre.

www.ingramcontent.com/pod-product-compliance
Lightning Source LLC
Chambersburg PA
CBHW051643160426
43209CB00004B/771